"Giving birth, there is no kn____ing, it takes courage"

Congratulations!
With love
Marie
:)

THE
SMART WOMAN'S
GUIDE TO

GIVING
BIRTH

Mind, body and birth
partner preparation for
people short on time
and attention span.

BY MARIE J. TAYLOR

First published 2019

Published by Forward Thinking Publishing

A catalogue record for this book is available from the British Library.

ISBN: 978-0-9934652-4-6

For Jack and Douglas,
my favourite adventurers

Contents

Conscious Mind

Unconscious Mind

Environment

Body Training

Body Nourishment

Birth Partner

Introduction

In this book are all the things that I wish someone had told me before my babies arrived. It's the stuff I wish I'd realised earlier when I look back on my difficult first birth, then again at my triumphant experience with baby number two, and even after that when I'd trained as a specialist birth supporter known as a doula.

Since then I have witnessed that so much knowledge and understanding about motherhood comes from word of mouth. Either from other mothers or passed down from mothers to daughters.

If, like me, you have an imperfect set up with your own mother, perhaps you live a long way from her, or you simply don't get on, then there might be a gap between what you know and understand of your body's innate wisdom about giving birth.

Another challenge in modern society is that birth is hidden away, behind hospital doors, so we are less familiar with the knowledge, trust and experience that our great grandmothers had. This book attempts to bridge that gap too. I share information about birth and also ways to understand how people really tick (and by people that most definitely includes you).

There are bookshelves already filled with diagrams to learn about the physical aspects of pregnancy and birth - yet the more subtle mental and emotional 'opening' process that new parents experience is so individual that it makes it difficult to map out.

This book will help you practise trusting in the way you feel. You are not broken or wrong. How you feel in the process of pregnancy and birth (and life actually) is like a trail of breadcrumbs leading you to something to help you grow as a person.

Contained in the following pages is a unique blend of what I learned from my own very different birth experiences, and then my training to be a doula. It's blended with over fifteen years' experience as a life coach, supporting people to recognise when they are getting in their own way, then helping them to overcome past trauma, develop a successful mindset and start to get the results they truly want.

Complete the foundation classes first

The book is designed so that you complete the foundation classes first, then you can dip in and out of the 42 bite-sized pieces of wisdom as you move along your pregnant journey. The earlier you read this book in your pregnancy the better because some pieces of wisdom need to be implemented or practised in order to help you.

However, if you're like I was during my first pregnancy, with very little time to prepare, just knowing a handful of the tips inside this book will help you and baby have a gentler arrival to motherhood, parenthood and life.

The reason I wrote this book is because I am on a mission; to bridge the gap between the modern mainstream understanding of birth with the latest appreciation of the significant effect it can have on our mental wellbeing and reconnect you to the forgotten wisdom from our great grandmothers that used to get handed down from generation to generation. I also want to lay out the practical help and wisdom of all the women, midwives, hypnobirthers, doulas and authors of all the books I wish I'd read before I'd given birth, instead of being busy working on my career.

An unknowingly miss-able opportunity.

I began by helping fellow mums in the school playground with the understanding and knowledge in this book and now I'd like to serve you too.

Please take from my personal experience only what is right for you. Nothing in here comes close to a substitute for professional medical advice and should never be treated as such. Always consult a medical practitioner for medical advice and I advise that all birthing women have a midwife and a doula by your side if you can.

Ultimately though, you know you best. You also know your baby the best. My intention with sharing the knowledge contained in this little book is that you'll learn to trust yourself and that quiet voice inside your head which is sending you wisdom all the time.

Trusting yourself sounds easy but it's not. It may mean that you seek more than one professional opinion from time to time or you might have to have a difficult conversation with someone. The thing to remember is that you don't get this time back so if in doubt go all out. Ultimately, I learned that the more you prepare, the smoother your journey will be. The more you ignore things, the worse they get until they are dealt with.

The quality of your life is determined by the quality of the questions you ask yourself.

Birth requires us to strip back on the excesses of modern life, whether they are fashions or trends because birth is a process that's thousands of years old. You'll begin to notice that parenting makes you live from that deep down place. You know, deep down, when you know it'll be OK, or deep down if there's something not quite right.

Science, technology, and any over-thinking gets superseded in this experience, forcing you back to the real you. It forces you back to your truth about what is and is not okay for you.

Sometimes we edit or deny who we really are or only show a certain version of how we feel. Maybe we put on airs and graces or play down aspects of our greatness. But becoming a mother is like a quest we watch in the movies, that is real and it will 'out' any façades or strategies you might have used before.

I remember my teacher describing birth and parenting as wearing your heart on the outside. Actually, I think that's a good description of the first ten years of parenting.

In the process of becoming a mum, that begins at the earliest moments of pregnancy, you get presented with so many opportunities to choose: either choose to overcome and grow beyond your current plateau, limitation or fears, or choose to gloss over and deal with it another day.

Birth is a needle moving moment that, from where you stand now, that you can't fully comprehend yet. It's a bit like me explaining to you how a strawberry tastes. The only way to truly understand its sweet and juicy flavour is by tasting it yourself.

However, when you look back over time, when you watch others on the same quest, my intention my friend, is that you are glad you took my hand here.

Marie

Class One

The Beginning

When we discover we are pregnant, whether planned or unexpected, we can feel quite isolated. Even if there are plenty of loving people around you, being the pregnant person gives us a very different perspective to everyone else. Our unique view needs to be respected and accommodated and it can seem completely different to any life situations that have shown up before, which is unsettling.

The morsels of wisdom on the following pages have been lovingly collected to help you discover ways to navigate this pretty rare adventure. During pregnancy and throughout this book you reveal and rediscover what is uniquely true for you.

No matter how many of the suggested exercises you do, no matter how many things you remember about what is contained within the pages of this book, now is a time when you should feel like a queen. Not someone for whom allowances should be made, but someone who should be revered. And if you're not feeling that way, the number one thing to do is find people and an environment where people desire that for you too. This is not an experience to do alone. Evolution created it that way on purpose.

In birth, like in life, you are more likely to be successful if you get a clear picture of how you want it to go. If you have only ever experienced scenes of childbirth from TV and film (like One Born Every Minute on Channel 4 or What To Expect When You're Expecting) remember everything has to be dramatic in TV and film in order to justify the screen time. I recommend that you go to YouTube and watch some great examples of what a positive birth experience looks like. Visit my website **www.urbanearthmother.com** for some links.

What you'll notice that the common attributes of these examples show women in quiet, dimly lit, private, safe, secure surroundings. They are supported by people who believe in them and who aren't compromised by other people or agendas that can often be the practical reality of operating a large organisation.

If you're like me though, I wouldn't have felt safe giving birth at home, so I birthed in a hospital. While I was there we strived to achieve a similar environment and to have what felt right for me, baby, and dad.

EXERCISE

So now let's put this into action. The following three questions will help you begin to think about things that may not have occurred to you before.

Question 1: Who do you already know who makes you feel good? To help your ideas flow consider friends, family, work colleagues, church, clubs or people on courses you've taken.

Question 2: What preferences do you currently have about your experience, your partner's and your baby's birth?

Question 3: How do you want to feel afterwards?

Getting Organised

Sometimes we just don't want to make a fuss. We're pregnant, not ill right? But good prep for giving birth requires you to spend some time on it. Preferably not the 'binge watching boxsets' kind of time, but regular consistent training, like martial arts in the dojo' kind of time.

So if you do have time, schedule a regular 30 minute slot, put a daily timer on your phone, so that you can absorb everything in this book. (And put a copy in the loo so you can guarantee you'll be reminded to pick it up each time you pay a visit).

What if I have no time?

I get it. When I was giving birth the first time I had no 'spare' time. This is exactly why this book doesn't have any fluff or padding so you can get straight to the top tips here. Also, when I was pregnant, I had the attention span of a gnat.

For these reasons the book is designed so you can either choose pages at random each day or you can decide to learn one thing every day for six weeks or learn six things every day for a one week. It's up to you and all depends on how long you've got to prepare.

Question 4: Decide a regular time of day to focus on preparing for giving birth and set a timer to remind you. What time did you decide?

In my experience most people's minds seem to get focused and start to comprehend the reality of the actual birth and parenthood at around week 30.

- You have enough time to ramble through and practise the tips contained in this book. Just give yourself 30 minutes a day to study or practise, be still and create space in your day for your baby's arrival. You'll make the transition to motherhood much easier if you do.

- There is definitely not enough expertise in this book to replace your amazing doctor, midwife and health professionals who are crucial members of your support team as you go through this brand new and unfamiliar process. In my own story, had I not asked the advice of my health professionals, about what I thought was a lingering cold, they wouldn't have been able to save my life. If something is bothering you, something feels not quite right, do not hesitate to ask them, or ask repeatedly if you need to.

For some of the techniques and exercises it's a good idea to practice and get really good at them. If you learn better by watching and listening than reading, I've created a series of classes online that teaches everything in this book in just seven classes. More information is available at **www.urbanearthmother.com**

To recap, what you've already considered here:

Question 1: Who do you already know who makes you feel good? To help your ideas flow consider friends, family, work colleagues, church, clubs or people on courses you've taken.

Question 2: What preferences do you currently have about your experience, your partner's and your baby's birth?

Question 3: How do you want to feel afterwards?

Question 4: Decide a regular time of day to focus on preparing for giving birth and set a timer to remind you. What time did you decide? (Write it on a post-it note and put it on your bathroom mirror).

Now you are beginning to place focus on the things you want in order to have a gentle birth and relaxed transition to parenting. In the next class we explore things in a little more depth.

Class Two

There were six areas that I was paying attention to during my second pregnancy that lead up to my amazing and triumphant experience of giving birth. These were:

Two aspects of your mind:

- Your conscious mind (the fact checker part of your brain)
- Your unconscious mind (the place where all feelings are coming from and also where memories are stored and the control centre for your body)

Two aspects of your body:

- Nourishing your body
- Training your body

Two aspects of your birth 'climate':

- Training and finding a great birth supporter
- Creating a great birth environment.

Two aspects of your mind: conscious and unconscious

Your conscious mind and unconscious mind work very much together. Think of them a bit like the captain of a ship (conscious mind) and the crew (your unconscious mind). The captain decides the destination you're heading for. The unconscious mind is the crew that does all the micro tasks that actually make that happen.

For example; if you consciously (and on purpose) decide to nod your head, it is your unconscious mind that actually deals with how far to move each of the muscles and ligaments involved as well as the necessary adjustments to your balance throughout the rest of your body. You don't have to think about the mechanics of this; there is no involvement from your conscious mind.

Your conscious mind on the other hand is fed by information. The key thing to know about the influence of your conscious and unconscious minds is that all learning (and change) all happen at the unconscious level.

Feeding your conscious mind information is needed to acquire enough new knowledge so that you can feel confident that you know what you are doing. You then practice making that knowledge become a skill.

And finally, your unconscious mind is where 'feeling confident' actually happens and where the things you learn become automatic (and unconscious) once learnt - think for example of when you learn to drive, everything is directed by the conscious mind. Think about all the things you do to change gear. To start with you consciously remember to press the clutch then move the gear stick. Once it is 'learnt' you automatically do it without thinking.

Two aspects of your body: nourishment and physical training

Like a marathon, birth is a significant physical event. You have to work up to it, not just show up on the day. Marathon runners do plenty of training before the big day and birth is no different. Some of that training is to do with physical strength and some of it is to do with practising mental and emotional strength, like how to deeply relax. Some people need more practise than others.

If there was any time to have a body in tip top condition, then pregnancy and birth is it! You may not have paid much attention to the messages your body has given you before, (I know I certainly hadn't) but when you eat too much of the stuff it struggles to deal with and you're pregnant, or you over do it physically, the effects are amplified. Inside this book you will find signposts to food or activities that support your body as it goes through different stages.

Two aspects of your birth climate: support team and environment

Finally, the last sections in this book are about things outside of you. These are your birth support team and the place where you decide to birth your baby. These are key ingredients of a triumphant birth.

A great birth supporter who knows you and knows just what to do to support you when you are under pressure was the second most important part of the triumphant birth I had with my son. (The first was the confidence in my ability to do it).

Consideration about the environment surrounding the birth was something I never considered properly first time around. The reality was that in the end there wasn't much scope for choice as I was having complications so I was following medical advice. However, if I had known the things contained in these pages I believe it would have made the whole process of birth easier (and potentially could have prevented the emergency situation occurring in the first place).

EXERCISE

An introduction, experiment and test drive for your unconscious mind

A story...

Imagine a painter who paints two exact same pictures, of the exact same images with the same colour paints. For one she uses a white canvas and the other a green. Even with the same picture, artist, paint and brush strokes the result is massively different depending on the backdrop.

So even though you have the same biology and are giving birth the same way that millions of women have done before you, the canvas you have is unique to you; to the beliefs about your strengths, weaknesses and family traits, which affects the thoughts you have, the feelings you feel and subsequently the choices you make. Your physiology is unique and so is the anatomy of your mental and emotional blueprint. We don't only inherit our eye colour from our parents and grandparents who've lived before us.

So before I introduce you to your unconscious mind first let's break down what is actually happening in each moment of your experience.

Before words are spoken, there is a thought. Before the thought, there is a feeling which is a reaction to what you notice about any given experience.

14

At various moments, thoughts may reinforce (as evidence for) a pre-existing belief, or a thought can cause you to create a new belief. All these beliefs cannot remain in your conscious awareness all the time, so they are stored away in your unconscious mind which is a kind of 'belief bank'. This means that if ever you need the beliefs or knowledge in the future, they are in a place that a instantly accessible to you.

Sometimes inside your unconscious mind, your 'belief bank' resembles a kitchen cupboard that's never been cleared out. You know what I'm talking about. Some of those tins at the back are well beyond their best before date, some of these are the equivalent of beliefs you formed early on in life, sometimes even as early as birth. These beliefs served you at one point in your life, but things might be different now and you will have developed skills and had experiences that mean you don't need to keep them if they aren't supporting you to get the result you want. This means the effort you are making NOW to support you and your baby's entry to the world is so important. Let's test it out.

Do this simple experiment:

Until the moment you read this you weren't thinking consciously about the colour of your front door, but now you are. It's as easy as that to access your unconscious mind.

Do that experiment again: Now bring to mind an event when you were really happy and laughing.

Finally, do that experiment again: Imagine you are walking on a sandy beach, feel the sand between your toes and warm water from the sea coming up to meet your feet. Notice the warmth of the sun on your body.

Did you notice your breath slowed as you thought of this relaxing scene?

This was a demonstration about understanding how to use your unconscious mind to get you the result you want. When your focus shifted and your breath slowed, you relaxed more. Managing your mind is the key to success in all areas of life. A key part of being able to do this consistently is by clearing out your unconscious mind like you'd clear a kitchen cupboard of all the things that are no longer of any use.

Doing this before baby arrives means you will improve the possibility of success you'll experience in all areas of life, not just the transition to parenthood - because so much of how we behave is governed by how we feel, and what we feel is governed by what beliefs we walk around with.

This is the equivalent of creating a canvas that you, the artist, wants to create on. The same events create a different result depending on the different backdrop on to which you paint all your experiences on.

Congratulations! This is the end of your foundation classes. Now let's get into the practical stuff.

Conscious Mind

Labour like a surfer.
Contractions arrive like a wave.
They build to a peak, then there is a rest.
Imagine you are surfing.
See how long you can stay on the wave.

Labour like a surfer

There are three stages of a normal labour. Here are the basics.

Stage one has mini stages. These are "early labour", "active labour" and "transition". First there is "early labour" which could last days. Then comes "active labour". After that comes a "transition" as you progress to Stage two.

At the point of "transition" the cervix (which is a muscle) opens to about 10cms in diameter which is the width of a standard sized Easter egg.

Stage one contractions (that have started naturally without induction) start small and grow in intensity. As you start to notice them arrive, imagine you are a surfer catching a wave, and once the contraction arrives see how long you can 'surf' that wave.

There may be a gradual loss of the ability to speak as a contraction arrives (as you approach active labour), then it returns again during the moments of rest between contractions.

Stage two is when you 'push' or if you're one of those people who doesn't need to push and can simply 'breathe' your baby out with breaths (from the diaphragm).

Concentrate on your out breath while having the contraction. By making low sounds at the same time, the diaphragm supports the downward motion of the contraction. (Try making a long low noise now, you can feel the diaphragm move downwards.)

Stage three is the period after baby has emerged. Once baby has arrived the placenta - that has been the bridge between mother and baby throughout the pregnancy - is also 'birthed'. Contractions start again to make this happen, which might take up to an hour after baby is born.

If you birth in a medical environment they may encourage you to have a medical intervention to speed this process up. This is something to research and think about when you write your Birth Plan.

After the placenta is delivered, the focus shifts to the umbilical cord which is clamped and cut. Make sure everyone waits long enough for all of baby's blood to leave the placenta and reach their body. The cord looks white when that has happened.

Please note, guidelines in hospitals change all the time and not all birth settings wait until the cord is white. To help make sure this happens you could request that your birth supporter cuts the cord and you can tell them to take their time and wait until the cord has turned white. (It might take 20 minutes before the cord goes white).

Some parents choose to have what is called a Lotus Birth. The umbilical cord is not cut in a Lotus Birth and baby is left attached to the placenta until the cord separates naturally. This usually 3-10 days after baby is born. This can be a challenging thing to do in our modern lives. Advocates of the lotus birthing method believe infants are put under unnecessary stress when they are cut off from the placenta and the living environment that they have been used to is changed dramatically and too quickly.

Prostaglandins + Relaxin help labour
Adrenaline does not

How labour starts

When baby is ready, their adrenals send a message to the mother's pituitary gland in the brain that baby is now ready to be born. The dance of the mother and baby begins. Hormones called prostaglandin and relaxin drive the whole process.

Together, these hormones cause tissues to soften so there is more 'give' in the body and therefore increase flexibility to give birth.

Remember, changes in your physical body are reflected in your mental and emotional state. For some women softening is easy both physically and mentally, for others it's not easy. You should make sure you have an alert and well prepared birth supporter who knows you well so they can help create an environment where you soften easily and you can let baby out.

Hormones affect feelings
Feelings effect hormones
It's a circle
If labour isn't progressing it's good to know how to
increase your oxytocin levels.

Hormone of love

Hormones in your body make you feel a certain way. The vice versa is also true. Feeling a certain way affects what hormones run through your body.

The more of the hormone oxytocin you create, the easier giving birth will be. Oxytocin is the fuel of birth. You've experienced oxytocin flowing in your body before. You feel the effects of it when you feel 'in the mood' for love. It's present when you make love, (and when you have contractions and breastfeed).

If labour isn't progressing it's good to know how to increase your oxytocin levels.

The thing to remember is that oxytocin won't share any limelight with adrenalin. They are like oil and water, so removing all stress or causes of stress is the first step.

Your environment is the key: dim lighting, soft music, privacy, a sense of touch, basically the same things that got you 'in the mood' to create the baby is the mood you need to recreate to help baby come out.

You need to feel totally safe physically, and free from other people's wishes or agendas taking priority. In privacy and not pressured, you can stay aware of your instinct and your body.

(This is also why midwives recommend that you tweak the nipples to help raise oxytocin levels).

You cannot run feelings of 'miserable' if you strike
a powerful joyful pose.
Test it: Lift your chin up, put on a wide smile,
with cheering arms in the air.
All feelings have a physical response.
Even if you have to 'fake it' it still has an effect.

All feelings have a physical response

You can test this now. Feel happy for a moment. Think of something that made you really happy. Great.

Now think of something that makes you feel sad, really feel it, just for a moment, and notice where in your body did you notice the differences? Also notice what change happened to your breath.

Sometimes we don't even realise how we're feeling, but someone who knows us well can tell when a feeling or a thought turns up for us. It affects your body. Be aware of how this could be helping or hindering baby coming out. It's good to know what you could change to help you physically.

Check in to your body now. Start at your feet and work up. Is there any tension in your feet? Legs? Hips? Anywhere else?

Do you need to do something to clear the tension - a conversation, a dance around the living room, a belly laugh, or a good rant? Speaking the word 'Yes' repeatedly, either in your head or out loud might help your body focus on moving forward with the process of birth.

EXERCISE

Start with your feet, tense all the muscles in your feet for a moment, then release and relax them while breathing out. Move up your body to each area in turn. Tense your calf muscles, then release them. Tense your thigh muscles then release them (and so on). This tense then release technique can help you relieve tension you weren't even aware that you might be holding. (Some hypnotherapists use this technique to start a session).

From the firmness of your nose to
the softness of your lips

Transition

During labour, once the cervix has opened to 10cm, (what they call 'fully dilated') it transforms from the firmness of your nose to the softness of your lips, (a bit like softly set jelly).

After the early stages of labour when oxytocin is the main hormone involved, things begin to change. As the moment of birth becomes more imminent, there is a sudden increase in adrenaline level which activates the foetal ejection reflex. You may experience a sudden rush of energy; maybe be upright and alert, with a dry mouth and shallow breathing and perhaps have the urge to grasp something.

As the hormones flowing around your body switch, you may express fear, anger, or excitement, and the new flush of hormones can cause several very strong contractions, so baby can be birthed quickly and easily.

There is a short period as this switch takes place when you will have both oxytocin and adrenaline running through your body. This might cause confusion or you might ask yourself, 'can I do this?'. Sometimes this shows up as 'Do I ask for medication/pain relief drugs or something similar?'

Rely on your birth supporter as someone you can trust, who will tell you honestly and supportively, how well you are doing, because at that moment you might not be sure.

It's the equivalent of cheering crowds at sporting events, the good support keeps you moving. In giving birth, this is the moment that other people can help carry you forward.

EXERCISE

Think for a moment about a time when you were doing something and you began to doubt yourself or wonder whether you could keep going? If you can't remember a time like that, set yourself a small physical challenge and pay attention to the pattern of thoughts and feelings that come up for you. Maybe you could climb the stairs ten times and watch your thoughts as you do it.

For a longer-term experiment, to see how you behave over time, you could start a new routine like keeping a food diary for a week. This helps you notice what you say to yourself if you stick to it or what you say to yourself when you don't.

The way we do one thing tends to be the way we do many things.

The point of the exercise here is to stay aware of how your mind influences how you handle the new routine and how you handle sticking to a new challenge.

Understanding "Optimal Foetal Positioning"
is like knowing how to get a tight polo neck
jumper over your head easily.

Baby turns to exit

Babies can only navigate the space they have and that is affected by the way you move and hold yourself most of the time. Have you ever tried putting on a polo neck jumper that is a little too tight? If you don't position it right from the start, you'll struggle to get it on. You'll still do it, but it's more difficult. Understanding this next tip will assist you in birth because this is one of those things that you may not have thought about before.

You see, to get a polo neck jumper on you must first put it over the crown or the back of your head. This is true of womb exiting babies too (some come out star gazing too - this is what's called a 'posterior baby').

Womb-exiting babies have to do the equivalent of the 'double salco' in ice-skating terms in order to get out, so listen to suggestions from your birth professional about positions to try.

While you're pregnant wherever possible choose to sit on a yoga ball instead of the sofa to help everyone to have a good starting position.

Babies can only navigate the space they have and that is affected by the way you move and hold yourself most of the time.

When you take responsibility for something does it feel joyful or like a burden?

Remember B.R.A.I.N.

Responsibility

The most fulfilling and proud moments of a job well done are when we know that WE are the cause of the success. The source of that pride comes from our overcoming of obstacles, that we figured it out and that we did it, ourselves.

You have an opportunity to feel triumphant in giving birth as it offers a chance for you to learn (maybe for the first time), how strong and wise you really are. Birth gives you an opportunity to discover how robust and resilient your body can be, all without any conscious effort from you.

Sometimes we feel fighty or find fault with others when we think we are taking responsibility for something. Beware of pointing the finger or the flip side which is handing responsibility for your success to someone else.

In the moments of giving birth though, things can move quite fast so remembering this acronym can help you and your birth supporter make informed decisions.

B What are the **benefits** of the proposed treatment or intervention or this decision?

R What are the **risks associated** *with this decision?*

A Is there an **alternative** and if so what is it, what are the risks and benefits of those? Is there an alternative that maybe isn't available here, but somewhere else?

I What does your **intuition** and your partner's *instincts* tell you to do?

N **Next or Nothing.** What comes next if we say yes? What happens if we do *nothing?*

EXERCISE

What could you do differently to create things the way you want them? Sometimes that means speaking up and saying what is not okay for you. Sometimes it's figuring out what you want rather than what you don't want. Here's the thing many people miss. If you don't know what you want, that is okay. It's good to ask someone who has done it before for ideas about what you could do or have. The important point to note is that by taking responsibility for yourself and your experience this does not mean you have to do it all by yourself.

The key is to be clear about what you want in terms of how you want to feel.

Decide what you will and won't accept and stick to it.

And now having made that decision, try dropping it and shrugging your shoulders to see what it feels like to walk without any expectations at all.

Sometimes we pick up beliefs and expectations from others that are now out of date, misinformed or just not right for us as individuals. Be open minded and feel into what is right for you.

Unconscious Mind

Thoughts become things

Reveal your blindspots

The only way to find out what deep beliefs you hold about birth is to take a good look. Just like you weren't consciously thinking about the colour of your front door until I just drew your attention to it, all your beliefs are in your mind, all the time, in your unconscious and they run without any awareness or direction from you.

With practice you can begin to see your own blindspots, but it is easier for others to help us see them. You don't need anyone to get started straight away though.

Start with the following exercise.

EXERCISE

This will reveal if there are any beliefs running in your unconscious that aren't currently supporting a gentle and enjoyable birth.

You will need:

A timer
A pen and two sheets of A4 paper

Method:
Set the timer for 20 minutes. Aim to fill at least a side of A4

paper per question. Write down everything and anything that comes to mind when you to complete the following sentences.

When you do this, pay particular attention to the surprising or unexpected things that pop into your mind and notice any memories that you haven't recalled for a long time too. (This is usually where I help my life coaching clients make a small change that makes the most difference).

1. Birth is...
2. Birth is not...
3. Parents are...
4. Parents are not...

If you and your partner do this, you'll realise the differences in beliefs that two (even close) people can hold. Beliefs can change (or be changed) to support you to get the results and the experience that you want. This isn't about who or what is right, it's about being curious about what's going on at a deeper level for you.

Focus on what you want.
Don't Think Of A Black Cat

Focus on what you want

Notice what happened when you just read 'don't think of a black cat'. In order for your mind to follow the instruction, it had to first think of a black cat so that it could then make some representation in your mind of 'not' thinking of a black cat.

Why is this important? You just proved to yourself that the mind cannot process negatives. Each time you think of a negative or a 'not' of something, you actually create it in your mind as something to focus on. This, in turn, increases the likelihood of it happening.

That said, there is some merit in knowing what you don't want though. It is sometimes a good place to start. Once you've given plenty of space to thoughts about what you don't want, eventually, your heart's desire and what you really want can bubble up to the surface so you are more aware of it.

Vulnerability has many faces

Vulnerability

Waves of vulnerability go through you at different times in pregnancy, and it doesn't discriminate between circumstances. Sometimes that feeling is telling you that you need to get the hell out of there. Other times these feelings show up to remind you how strong you are or remind you to remove some 'dead wood'. It might be that you need to reassess the relationships that will surround you and the child after birth.

I've heard the feeling of vulnerability described as being "uncoated". It's not always obvious to us that we're feeling vulnerable. Sometimes it feels or looks like something else. For example, perhaps you are finding something challenging, unjust or something else? Wonder for a minute if feeling vulnerable could be the real root of any problems that pop up for you.

By the way, it's okay to feel vulnerable. It's completely understandable. There are no rules to pregnancy, life or birth. Sometimes life feels more comfortable when there are.

If you're feeling vulnerable ask yourself, what needs to happen to help you relax about this situation now?

EXERCISE

Grab a pen and paper. The following guided meditation is designed to reveal areas in your unconscious where you may feel vulnerable so that you can just be aware or perhaps resolve them. Either record yourself reading it aloud and or there's a recording of it you can listen to on my website **www.urbanearthmother.com**

Allow yourself to take a moment to relax. Put distractions to one side as they come into your mind and gently switch off your thinking brain. Notice the ground and the feeling of your body being supported by the floor underneath you. Get comfortable. Sit or stand on the floor however you can feel comfortable now.

Deepen and double your sense of relaxation and soften your body and soften your mind one breath at a time. We will begin by focusing on your out-breath. Every breath out is an opportunity to let go. Let the in-breath come in easily. And relax into the natural rhythm of your breathing. Breathe a bit deeper, breathe into your belly and allow your body and you to take up a little more space.

Trusting in the wisdom of your body, when you are ready, ask yourself, what do you need? Is it someone knowledgeable to be with you? Is it space? Someone to guard your corner perhaps? Someone to make sure your wishes are followed and someone who can be relied on to know if your plans need to be modified?

What do you need to feel totally safe and supported? Do you have enough knowledge about the physiological process you are facing, or do you need more trust in your body. Do you need to cultivate a belief that you can do this?

Perhaps you need others to change the words they use around you so you feel cherished.

When you have answers to these questions for self-enquiry go on and ask yourself more...

What choices do you already know you have to make that you haven't taken yet? Do you need to know that you are allowed to take more time to think things over and ask more questions? Or is it something else?

Wait for things to bubble up to the surface of your mind. Trust into the wisdom of your body. Breathing, letting go, surrender.

If you feel some discomfort breathe into the heart of it, what is it here to guide you towards or away from, to learn or soften about? Once you get the learning, be willing in this moment to release it with each out breath. Allow a pause to exist before the breath comes in, breathe, let mind and body keep emptying out, moving together, let it come through you.

And now as you bring your awareness back to come back into the room, ask yourself, if you were queen, with no limits, what would you arrange so that you can relax now?

Write down whatever comes to mind.

"Fear is just excitement without the breath."

Fabulous not fearful

Childbirth is an event of great and often underestimated power. One that you can only really comprehend after the event. So, if fear ever shows up the best antidote is to always to take action.

Often though we become paralysed by fear. One way to no longer be afraid of experiences in front of us is to do a rehearsal; it might be mental preparation, physical, emotional or even practical. Local antenatal classes or hypnobirthing classes could be good for you.

For now, investigating counts as taking enough action.

What happens when you feel fear? Do you shrink, lash out, freeze, fawn or do you do something else?

It's a common belief that your body is a reflection of your consistent thoughts which sets it, a bit like a thermostat. The way to squash fear is to change the thermostat by gaining knowledge and understanding. If you can't achieve that by yourself, find people who have the ability to give you the knowledge you need that will help you dissolve your fear.

Perhaps for you that will be your doctor, midwife, doula, maybe a family member or is it someone else?

Also consider what thermostat might have been set for you while you were in the womb? If you have any fear, what is that really about, are your fears really real or just habit?

If you give fears some time and space so you can really examine the roots of them, often they begin to evaporate or the real issue bubbles up from underneath. Deal with the real issue or the purpose of the fear and it will evaporate. Remember if you get 'stuck' in fear tell your health professional what's going on so they can support you to get out of it.

EXERCISE

1) List 3 fears about birth, then 3 fears about being a parent.

2) If these fears are based on a belief about a limit of your ability or character, what evidence can you find that this belief may be just a little bit false?

3) Ask your birth supporter to give you an example of when they've witnessed that your fearful belief was not true.

4) Take some deep breaths, then if you do have fears or worries explore them in more depth.

- When I think about pregnancy, do I have any worries or fear?

- When I think about birth what's my worry?

- When I think of the baby what's my worry/fear?

Note: You don't have to 'fix' all your fears, simply knowing what they are is often enough. Just notice them.

Joy: What is your limit?

Joy: what's your limit?

Joy is happiness super charged. Take this as your personal reminder that you ARE allowed to feel joy and be supercharged happy.

When you think of something that makes you feel joyful, imagine and double the size of that feeling. Savour every moment just like when you take time to taste a perfectly ripened juicy strawberry. These moments are the ones we pursue and we can only receive them if we stop, sit, breathe and connect with what is happening in this moment and let all the goodness in.

Receive the goodness and the joy that is available to you.

EXERCISE

Take just two minutes of your life right now and sit. Placing one hand on your heart and one on your belly. Imagine an egg-shaped circular flow of love from around your heart to around your baby and back again. Breathing out through the mouth, focus on the out-breath as you would during a contraction, and notice your thoughts.

If you experience something that is not Joy just make a mental note of it, thank the part of you that brought your attention to it, and promise yourself that you will do your best to address it (after this exercise). Write it down if you need to and search for a glimpse of the joyous connection available to you now between you and your child.

- How happy do you allow yourself to be? Out of ten?

- Ask yourself, is it okay for me to be really joyful and have things be easy for me?

- Ask yourself, is it okay for baby's experience to be joyful and really easy for them?

Did you get a definite 'Yes!' Or was it a 'sort of'? Anything less than a 'yes' suggests there's something to investigate there somewhere. Go deeper and ask yourself what's underneath that thought? What is that about and what purpose does it serve?

If you keep asking 'what the purpose is', of each answer your mind gives you, eventually you will know what you need address or let go of. Then when you whole heartedly can feel like 'it's okay for me to be really joyful and have things be easy for me' you know you've smoothed your onward path. You can unpick any bumps in the road by asking the same question until you get a resounding YES.

Sometimes things need to be believed to be seen

Birth is normal

When you hide something away, when you cannot actually see something, its 'story' can become different to the reality. Giving birth used to be an everyday occurrence in the community but now it mostly takes place in hospitals behind closed doors. This means that birth has become mostly unseen behind a protective frontline of hard-working health professionals.

Birth is completely normal. Do you believe that? The portrayal of birth on TV and film is quite the opposite. To make it to the final edit for a screen things have tended to be sensationalised or dramatised. As we absorb these messages it shapes our reality. That's why it's so important to check in with yourself about what you believe about your situation. What if that isn't really how it is? How might it be instead?

Visit **www.urbanearthmother.com** to find links to films other women have graciously shared of their normal births.

EXERCISE

This will reveal if there are any beliefs running in your unconscious mind that aren't congruent with the belief that birth is normal.

You will need:

A timer (for 3 minutes).

A pen and two sheets of A4 paper.

Step 1: Set the timer. Filling at least one side of A4 per question, write down everything and anything that comes to mind when you ask yourself to complete the following sentences. You should look out for any surprising or unexpected things that pop into your mind or any memories that you haven't recalled for a long time too. (These things are where a small change can make the most difference).

Finish the sentences:

- Pregnancy is. . .

- Pregnancy is not. . .

- Giving birth is. . .

- Giving birth is not. . .

If your first answers are not 100% positive your next task is to come up with answers that would be supportive of a gentle easy experience. This is like ordering new wiring for your brain. What positive way would you like these phrases to have come out, straight from your heart?

You get to decide what you believe is going to be true for you.

Zen
in
10 seconds
(or less)

Zen in ten

If negativity or worry ever tries to overwhelm you this is the thing to do. Practise it and you will find that it is impossible to hold a negative frame of mind when you do it. If you can do this for three minutes every day, by the time you're in labour you'll find it easy. When women tell positive birth stories many describe doing this instinctively anyway, using a candle flame to focus on rather than a spot on the wall.

EXERCISE

This technique is called Hakalau and comes from ancient Hawaiian practises.

1. Pick a spot on the wall to look at, above eye level, so that your field of vision seems to bump up against your eyebrows, but the eyes are not so high so as to cut off the field of vision. Imagine you're looking over a pair of spectacles.

2. "Let go." As you stare at this spot, just let your mind go loose, and focus all of your attention on the spot.

3. "Spread out." Staying focused on the spot let your jaw go loose and your vision begin to spread out.

4. Now, pay attention to the peripheral. In fact, pay more attention to the edges and your peripheral vision (rather than to the central part of your focus).

Stay in this state for as long as you can. Notice how it feels. Notice the relaxed or even ecstatic feelings that can begin to come to you as you continue to pay attention to the peripheral while keeping your focus steady.

This technique's official name is Hakalau. It comes from the ancient set of beliefs and practices designed to support well-being in Hawaii called Huna.

ENViRONMENT

Labour in water
Drink good water.

Water

There's a weird thing about water.

The benefits of labouring and birthing in water are well known, but according to a study less than 10% of births actually use it. One study found that water helps labouring women feel more comfortable and pain seems lessened.

"I think its weird that we don't use what we know works without side effects." (Professor Nicky Leap, Sydney University, Australia).

Reasons why more people don't use labour and birth in water could have to do with the number of people who choose to birth in hospitals and the logistics and resources involved with it. Staff in hospitals are often needed to care for a number of birthing women at the same time. Add to that, a hospital environment must be set up for emergency situations so they can respond quickly if they arise.

However, the majority of normal labours are not emergencies. A Birth Centre facility in Bristol, UK called Cossham Hospital has birthing pools in each room as well as double beds so that partners can stay comfortably even if labour takes a few days.

EXERCISE

- Ask yourself, if I want the option to labour and birth in water what am I going to need to organise in advance?

- Is there a birth centre available (nearby)?

- What facilities does it have? By choosing this what will not be available to us?

- Would I feel happier having my own birth pool and giving birth at home or would hospital be most comfortable for me?

"...Pain is never the sole creation of
our anatomy and physiology.
It emerges only at the intersection
of our bodies minds and culture".
(David B Morris, 1991)

Perspectives on pain

Imagine for a moment, the triumphant feeling of completing a marathon. It is only triumphant because of the ordeal you had to overcome to achieve it. The same comparison can be true of birth. Similarly, your attitude to pain affects your experience of it. The following are two different approaches that you might take.

The Pain Relief approach:

You ensure you have adequate pain relief, you 'don't have to be heroic', and you take the attitude that 'we should make full use of the benefits of modern technology. You'll probably make less noise and feel less agitated which helps you and staff if they are looking after more than one woman (which they often are in hospital environments).

The 'Working With Pain' approach:

You hold the belief that women can cope with the pain of uncomplicated* labour. Pain stimulates the body's natural opioids (pain relievers) so without it your body doesn't kickstart processes to help you be comfortable.

The Secret:

The secret that some people forget is that you don't have to stick to one approach if you don't want to. You are allowed to change your mind at any point.

At my second baby's birth, knowing I'd already had all sorts of medical interventions at my first birth, meant I gave myself permission to have any of those things again if I chose to. In the end, I didn't need them because circumstances were different and my belief in my ability to birth was much stronger. I also knew I didn't really want any of those interventions again, but I gave myself permission to accept assistance if it was necessary.

*There is a difference between 'normal' and 'abnormal' pain when the need for pain relief is associated with a baby in an awkward position. Speak to your midwife if you have questions about your individual experiences and circumstances.

How long is a pregnancy?
Hindu, Roman, or Aristotle

Induction

There are some interesting facts to know about due dates:

If you are Hindu or Roman, pregnancy lasts 9 months of 30 days = 270 days.

According to Aristotle, it lasts 10 lunar months of 28 days = 280 days.

Here in the west we either add 7 days and nine months to the first day of your last period = 277 days (which was actually only ever tested on 100 women as a theory.) Or we add 7 days and 9 months to the last day of your last period = 283 days. One study found that in a first pregnancy the average was more like 288 days.*

Due dates have become something people get really caught up with these days as we try to predict and control everything. The late Sheila Kitzinger, MBE, an outspoken campaigner for better maternity services, used to suggest that women lie at their first midwife appointment and add a week to your dates as a precaution to avoid any potential pressure to induce your labour if you don't want to.

Induction is the name of an intervention that starts things going instead of waiting for the baby's adrenals to send a message to the mother's pituitary gland that it is ready to be born.

If you are offered induction, you want to make a good decision about what is best for you personally and review the available evidence that's pertinent to your circumstances. You could ask your midwife to give you the evidence that supports induction for your particular circumstances, then you can make an informed decision.

Alternatively, if you need information about where to find evidence call or visit AIMS (the Association for the Improvement in Maternity Services) which is an independent organisation with a treasure trove of good information. It has a free and confidential helpline too. **(www.aims.org.uk)**

Something to bear in mind:

Induction is an intervention of a normal bodily process which might then create the need for further interventions following on from it. For this reason, you want to ask what might lie ahead for you if you take this first intervention are any more likely.

The great mystery
How long will you be pregnant?

When will baby arrive?

Jump-starting the mystery

Sometimes babies seem to prefer to stay right where they are and are not ready to come into the world. If yours is staying put, allow yourself in your mind's eye, to ask baby, "is there anything else you need me to do for you so that you are ready to be born soon?" Listen and pay attention to the quietest thoughts that pop into your head if you ask this.

Your intuition has a quiet voice so pay attention to what comes up even if it doesn't make sense at first and even if the thought is only fleeting at first. Write down thoughts that come to you once you've asked the question above. It could be that you can't arrange what you sense that baby wants or needs in the immediate moment, but a commitment made to doing so at a later date can often help things progress.

For great stories and examples of this check out the book Spiritual Midwifery by Ina May Gaskin. She retells a story of a baby who was reluctant to be born, labour stalled and it turns out baby wanted the parents to be married. The parents weren't concerned about marriage but they agreed to make it happen and labour progressed again smoothly.

Giving birth is a rare moment, and many mothers I've spoken to who were induced first time around, feel like they missed out on a big part of the experience. (My first birth was an emergency situation and I was medically induced. My second birth had no intervention at all and this is the option I'd prefer for every woman.)

I never felt like I missed out, but I did want to feel like I could give birth without the interference of medical drugs. Also, when I was induced the first time, my contractions went from gentle to really strong in a very short space of time which made me doubt myself, wondering if I was capable of giving birth if this was how it started, and not knowing how long I was going to have to keep this up. Without induction (with my second baby) I knew a lot of what's contained in this book and contractions started slowly and only got intense at the end. Plus I was more relaxed, my body and mind were in better shape, so my labour was shorter.

Therefore before choosing induction I recommend:

1. Get a good shoulder massage, often. There are acupressure points in the shoulder muscles that relate to the energy meridians connected to the liver and other parts which play a major role in getting things moving.

2. Check in with yourself and baby asking whether there are any emotional blockages (as above).

3. Go for at least two acupuncture treatments and ask the practitioner to prescribe a Chinese tea blend that is tailored to your needs.

You are in the presence
of a Goddess

No hustle no bustle

To birth easily, women in labour need to be relaxed physically and mentally. Sometimes in the moment (and in the excitement), this can get forgotten so remember:

- keep lights dimmed,

- keep other people's noise to a minimum,

- don't allow a lot of coming and going,

- just create as much peace as possible (whatever that looks like for you).

*Birth Where You Will
Be Most Relaxed*

Hospital or home?

Easy labours are most likely to happen when the mother is relaxed. This is more likely to happen if she knows the people around her when she is giving birth. The important thing to aim for is to be in a setting where you are relaxed wherever that may be. As part of your preparation for birth, getting good at relaxing will mean you can achieve it whatever the environment.

Did you know, in a study of 26,000 births in 2007 (called the Birthplace Study), 80% of women had not met the hospital staff who helped them, before their labour. What would that do for your level of relaxation? Would that be okay for you? Remember you'll be half naked to give birth. Let your caregivers know how you feel.

EXERCISE

The important thing in deciding where to birth your baby is to make a good decision for you. Pay attention to how you feel in different environments. If you are trying to decide where to give birth, go to each place, take a few moments so you can really notice how you feel when you are there.

- What do you say to yourself when you're there?

- What stops you doing what you want to do, when you are in each place?

- What do you find encouraging about each place?

By stating how you feel, wherever you decide to birth, you do not need to attempt to solve, make sense or decide anything until you are ready to.

I can't decide

If you find you cannot decide, it's time to go a bit deeper. The following might seem like odd questions at first, requiring a bit brain twisting, but if you were doing coaching with me to help you reach a deeper insight I'd ask you:

- If you were not deciding for a reason, what does 'not deciding' give you or mean for you? Also, what does 'not deciding' not give you and mean you don't have to do, that you don't want to do?

Knowing this kind of information also helps your supporters assist you better to make sure your needs and wishes are honoured properly.

Remember
B.R.A.I.N = informed consent

Informed consent

Often stuff happens at a birth and we get swept along with what the experts tell us we should do. Courses of action are suggested, and you often get asked to make a decision based on the facts you are presented with at the time.

If you're reading this book giving birth probably is not your area of expertise so the following questions are great to keep handy so you know you've asked good questions or at least some questions before consenting to what happens next.

1. Is this an emergency or do we have time to talk?

2. What would be the **benefits** of doing this?

3. What would be the **risks?**

4. What **alternatives** could we try first instead? Are there alternatives that aren't available here but somewhere else?

5. **If** we do this, what other procedures or treatments might we need as a result?

6. What would happen if we waited 20 minutes or an hour before doing it? What would happen if we did **nothing** at all? What comes **next** if we say yes?

Baby's tummy is the size of a Walnut!

Babies feed every two hours

Baby tummies are the size of a walnut so they don't stay full for long. While they need regular refills, you need peace and quiet so you can rest between the feeds, especially in the early days. Look at your environment and do what you can to make rest possible.

This is the number one reason why I was glad to get out of hospital. Hospitals aren't just busy at visiting times. Maternity wards are busy with doctors, midwives, paediatricians and maternity supporters who are all doing their rounds to make sure you and everyone else is well looked after. However, the problem this can cause is if you've only just fallen asleep, you can't control whether that is the moment the health professionals choose to come and talk to you.

Properly supported mothers really do recover more quickly. At home, a 'mother's help', doula or some other post-natal angel that can help with basic things like washing up or making lunch can be a total godsend in the first few weeks.

Another great time to arrange for this kind of help is after a week or so when (if) you have a partner about to return to work, who has been making lunch and tidying up.

BODY TRAINING

The breath and stillness:
a modern day challenge

The out breath

There are two types of breath to use during labour. Both use the same key piece of timing: that the out breath is always twice as long as the in breath.

Remember that ratio of 2:1 in the earlier stages of labour, making the out breath soft and focused, and twice as long as the in breath. For example breathe in for the count of four and out for a count of eight.

Practise doing 4 repetitions of this 2:1 breath is a good idea as this will last almost a minute, which is also how long early contractions last before they tail off and there's the period of rest in between.

As labour progresses, the muscles change from drawing up so the cervix dilates, to the uterus pushing down from the diaphragm, which helps baby on its way out. The breath that supports this process follows the same 2:1 ratio but because the out breath now has purpose and focus there is no need to count. The out breath is now more akin to the blowing out of a candle. As you draw power from the breath in, you imagine that you send the breath down and out, from the diaphragm.

EXERCISE

Take 5 minutes to practise this diaphragmatic breathing and focus on your out breath. This is a skill you will use during the birth.

Breathe

Practise every day to simply be, sit, breathe focus on slow deep breathing in and out. Set an alarm on your phone so you remember to do it. Every time you go to the toilet you can practise this down and out breath as going for a poo is almost identical to the feeling experienced in this active part of labour. (I never understood why nobody ever tells you that.)

If thoughts come into your mind while you are practising that is fine, notice them then bring your attention back to the breath.

Breathing deeply into the diaphragm so that the abdomen expands when you breath in actually gives the organs in there a massage as well as help the body perform its normal functions. The reason for this is that there's no 'heartbeat' to support the movement of lymph around the body so physical movement and diaphragmatic breathing helps the lymph and therefore toxins and white blood cells within it to move out of and around the body.

There is another benefit too. When you let go and relax your baby has more metaphorical space and can relax too. Relax and allow yourself to spend some time to get to know each other, expand in to the softness of you and take the time to be curious about who is this little being that's decided to spend some time with you.

*Making low noises helps baby because
the uterus is pushed down by the diaphragm
and your perception of pain is reduced*

Mama make some noise

You know all those polite manners you've been taught? "Keep the noise down." "Don't draw attention to yourself?" Get ready to take those rules and throw them out the window! Sounds easy right? For some people it might be.

It wasn't for me! If you've been raised as a people pleaser, well behaved, speak when spoken to you might struggle too. Practise making noise is the only solution.

The benefit of this is that many people also report that by making low noises you can reduce your experience of pain.

Physiologically this also helps baby wriggle out; by sustaining a longer firmer downward movement of your diaphragm. This gives baby something firm to push against.

EXERCISE

Your task is to get comfortable with your voice again. With one hand on your heart and one on your belly, make a low 'Ma' noise sound on the out breath. If you feel awkward making the sound keep practising until you do not feel self-conscious anymore.

Horizontal Half Hours

Sleep when tired

Do not put on a brave face.

The rule from now on is, sleep when tired. Granted it's not always easy to do. We might have busy full lives when we get pregnant and sometimes we don't notice when we're tired because we're busy just 'getting on with it'. It can feel like there's pressure to "just get on with it" too.

Remember nobody else is experiencing what you are experiencing. Rest is crucial, so make sure you're getting enough. Perhaps by setting a regular alarm, maybe on your phone, to remember to ask yourself whether you need a nap at 11am, 2pm, 5pm.

The key is to ask yourself regularly. Am I tired?

Don't do what I did! I ate so many biscuits taking myself on a sugar rollercoaster not realising that I was tired. I gained more weight than ever and probably caused complications because of it. In hindsight, instead I should have stopped work earlier and put my feet up for the last 8 weeks. If you aren't going on maternity leave because you worry about when you'll have to return to work, I would say that you can solve that problem if and when it arises, so don't waste energy on that concern.

Check as well, that you're not drinking more tea, coffee, eating chocolate or scoffing cake to give you a short-term sugar or caffeine boost if actually the real issue is that you need rest.

Growing a heart and nervous system for a new person every minute of every day without even thinking about it, takes energy. If you're struggling to make rest a priority ask someone to support you; tell the people around you to remind you and encourage you to rest. Even if you can't sleep, at the very least get horizontal for half an hour - this will not be as easy to make happen once baby arrives!

Loose lips above,
loose lips below

As above so below

Perineum Massage

This wisdom came straight from my own birth Doula. She told me, "As above so below and if you can loosen your lips enough to make a brrr sound, (breathing out through your lips), a bit like a neighing horse, then your body loosens in the whole pelvic area too".

Because birthing a baby requires a significant physical stretch many other cultures prepare for it in the final few weeks with a very specific perineum massage.

It is only ever done AFTER week 36. Ayurveda, the traditional Indian health approach uses techniques involving very specific technique and herbal preparations.

Remember to ask advice from your health professional about this or to investigate it further you can find information in the book 'The Gentle Birth Method' by Dr Gowri Motha, a highly regarded obstetrician and Ayurvedic doctor in London whose team has advised many A list celebrities before birth and supported them for the first few weeks once baby was born.

Having children will cause more running laughing and trampolining! Look after your pelvic floor!

Pelvic floor exercises

Do specific things to strengthen your pelvic floor to prevent a good, hard laugh or a sneeze push your bladder over the edge.

'Kegel', or pelvic floor exercises as they are commonly known, are one of the things you can do. They tone that area and help bring fresh circulation and nourish all the tissues in the pelvic region. If possible, do Kegel exercises three times a day (perhaps aligning them to some other activity like sitting at red traffic lights to help you remember).

They are not the only thing you can do though.

- Sit on chairs less.
- Swap your seat for a yoga ball.
- Sit in a squat position more often.

Actually, in China squatting is believed the best position to give birth in. They believe that baby will not have enough energy to birth if mother is laying on her back. While we are talking about birthing on your back, did you know that by being on all fours or squatting creates 33% more space than if a mother is lying on her back!

Is your body in alignment?

A clear route out

Babies turn during birth

Babies do the equivalent of a three-point turn during the process of being born. The actual route towards and out of the birth canal involves a number of twists so it helps if the route out is smooth and there's no anatomical 'potholes' to get stuck in.

A Bowen therapist, cranio-sacral therapist or osteopath can check whether your body and pelvis are in alignment. Like all complimentary therapy treatments, it could take 3 or 4 sessions to help the body maintain it's new 'settings'.

Here's a DIY check that you can do at home. Stand in front of a mirror with feet hip width apart and look at your shoulders. Are they the same height? If not, your pelvis could be out of alignment. Correcting this before birth could help baby get out more easily and your labour be gentler on both of you.

The smallest muscle exercises done every day can have a massive difference on your muscle tone

Bond with the ball

Sitting on sofas, looking at your mobile, playing on a tablet don't help maintain a healthy toned strong body. Modern comforts do nothing to help posture either.

Good tone and strength will help the process of giving birth and how fast you'll bounce back and recover afterwards. So sit on a yoga ball whenever you can.

The small movements required to keep you on the ball ever so gently gets those muscles and ligaments birth fit.

BODY NOURISHMENT

No wheat
No sugar
Especially in the final 4 weeks

No cake allowed

I was told by a highly regarded Ayurvedic doctor that:

- wheat can cause water retention in the muscles and
- sugar causes the ligaments of the body to lose their stretch.

Neither of these help an easy, gentle and enjoyable birth, which means if you are serious about your birth preparation then sadly you have to cut out the cake!

The cervix is a muscle that dilates and opens to 10cms wide when giving birth. It is the thing that midwives monitor in order to judge how things are 'progressing'. If you're not 'progressing' it might be that perhaps your muscles simply look that way because the cervix is puffy due to water retention. It might appear less dilated or be less able to dilate.

With my second baby I tried throughout the pregnancy to eliminate both wheat and sugar. It took a lot of practise. I eventually managed to achieve it in my last month (when it mattered the most). It took weeks of prep to find alternatives to my usual 'go to' foods.

The main contributor to my success was my self-imposed "apple before everything" rule. By sticking to a rule that I had to eat one small apple before I ate any snacks or unhealthy foods, I actually avoided any weight gain (that wasn't baby's).

EXERCISE

Planning is the key! Think of a breakfast, lunch and dinner that you already enjoy that does not contain wheat or sugar (and that includes things everything claiming to be 'sugar-free' that uses artificial sweetners too).

Yes, Yes, Yes

Yes: words have power

Say it (out loud)

The language we use has power and we can use it to support us and our progress. Say, 'Yes' over and over again and notice the subtle feeling of your body. Now say, 'No' over and over and notice what happens in your body. What was the difference? (Practise if you can't feel anything at first, it's subtle. 'Yes' causes us to expand).

What we say to ourselves (and others) creates a reaction inside and outside of us. In birth, if things start to slow down or stall there may be some emotional resistance going on that we can shift with a conscious use of language.

If you find things stalling while you're giving birth try simply saying the word "Yes" in your head (or out loud) over and over to see if it could cause your physiology to change and move things forward again.

You can smooth the path by asking yourself, what is the block here? What's that block trying to help me pay attention to and bring into my conscious awareness?

Don't worry if your mind's eye doesn't immediately serve up the answers to these questions. Sometimes they are just out of conscious reach, a bit like when you wake knowing that you just had a dream, but you can't seem to grasp or recall any of the details.

6 Medjool Dates or
Chocolate, Tea and Sleep

Eat dates

Pregnancy might be the first time you've actually thought about what you are eating. It was for me. I followed common sense advice that my Nan gave me as a child that, "a little bit of what you fancy does you good", and "everything in moderation".

Notice if you're craving sugary things, chocolate or caffeine as you might actually be tired and need to lie down and rest rather than satisfy that craving. Except when it's not. Except when that craving is because that's exactly what your body or mind needs. Only you can tell the difference.

To reduce my own sweet tooth I upped the amount of green veggies and oily fish I ate.

Magical Dates

Dates are a good source of protein, fibre and 'good sugar' (and they reduce cholesterol). There have also been small studies to investigate the old wives tale that eating dates can shorten labour. A study of two groups of women who ate six dates a day in the final four weeks of pregnancy and the other group did not, found that the date eaters had an 8.5 hours average first stage and the others averaged 15.1 hours*.

* Source: https://evidencebasedbirth.com/evidence-eating-dates-to-start-labor/.

Please note: this was not tested on women with gestational diabetes - you should always seek your own professional medical advice and eating dates is not a good idea if you have this condition.

Can't sleep?
Train yourself,
grab big pillows and a wet sarong

Guided meditation

Trouble sleeping at night is a common problem when you're heavily pregnant. So are complaints of feeling too uncomfortable or too hot.

Lower your temperature using this trick I picked up while backpacking in Sri Lanka. Run a sarong under the cold tap, wring it out and wrap your feet in it. It cools you just enough to help you sleep but doesn't make your bed damp nor make you too cold in the night that you wake yourself up.

You can also train yourself to sleep. Download a soothing guided meditation to your smartphone and listen to it everyday at bedtime. Eventually you will fall asleep and with practise your brain will associate sleep with the meditation music and you'll be able to use this as a trigger to help you fall asleep on an ongoing basis.

I use a meditation by Abraham Hicks called "Getting Into The Vortex".

Lovely, lovely lavender

Lavender: after the birth

Lavender* essential oil is the number one choice for adding to the bath after giving birth. It has delicate and harmonising scent that seems to agree with most people's senses. It's also regarded as having therapeutic benefits too.

It works wonders on the skin, has antiseptic qualities and is believed to help certain skin conditions and reduce inflammation. It is also thought to condition the body by relieving muscle aches and pains.

If you are a bit swollen or sore down below after giving birth, taking a bath with a drop of lavender essential oil can help you feel restored. One drop is enough. If you've got swelling or discomfort sometimes having your bath a bit cooler than usual can help give you some relief.

The sense of smell is often heightened in pregnancy. Simply smelling the aroma of this essential oil can calm and relax your mind and can help sleep too.

* Please note: Essential oils pack a powerful punch and NOT all essential oils are suitable for use while you are pregnant or breast feeding. Always read the label and seek professional advice.

Soup, Soup, Soup
Helps Clearing Out

Be kind to your digestion: before

According to Ayurveda, the ancient Indian approach to health and well-being, the final 12 weeks of pregnancy (called the last trimester) is all about clearing out.

To support the body to do this think about eating easy to digest foods. Go for clear soups and things that are packed with nourishment and are the opposite of stodgy stuff that clogs you up and are difficult for an already squashed digestive system to deal with.

Don't be obsessive about it though. Remember, a little of what you fancy does you good. Your body will present you with symptoms when things are out of balance. Stay balanced and pay attention to any signs your body gives you.

The added benefit of incorporating lots of soups into your weekly menu is that they are quick and easy to make too.

Porridge, Porridge, Porridge
Easy does it

Be kind to your digestion: after

Post partum means the period of time after giving birth. I have it on good authority that A list celebrities, who want to be "red carpet ready" in double quick time, employ the very best specialists in birth to support them for the first few weeks of motherhood (like a doula).

These doulas advise eating simple porridge for up to a whole week after baby is born. Gentle on the digestive system, it doesn't add any extra burden while you're recovering.

Another post partum tip from an Ayurvedic specialist that I received was about breast feeding. She told me to go easy on the quantity of salad that you eat because it can influence the breast milk you produce and result in making babies extra windy and uncomfortable.

A quick note about breast feeding

Breast feeding taking practise, if you're having difficulty getting the hang of it there are two great sources of support; your midwife or a La Leche Breast Feeding Support Worker **(www.laleche.org.uk).**

Birth Partner

How do you 'do' vulnerable?
How does your birth supporter 'do' vulnerable?
How do you 'do' scared?

Three questions on vulnerability

Both birthing mothers and birth supporters feel it.

Imagine…You get naked in front of lots of people who you don't know. They need to take a close look at parts of your body that people seldom take a close look at. You're not sure exactly what they're doing or why.

Logic says, it's natural to feel vulnerable.

So what happens when you feel this way?

What do you do or say to yourself?

What about your birth supporter? What happens when they feel vulnerable?

It could be that feelings of helplessness rise up. Maybe confusion? Uncertainty? Feeling under pressure? Some people try to befriend the person involved? These are all completely natural things to do.

If you are feeling vulnerable tell your caregiver and birth partner. Find your voice and when something comes up that you need support with tell your midwife.

Serve others from your saucer and not from your cup

Nurture

Imagine a cup and saucer. When the cup is being filled, any overflow collects in the saucer. If you serve people before your own cup is refilled at some point you will run out. This is never sustainable. Only serve others 'from your saucer and not from your cup'.

What's best for her IS best for everyone else

Now ask yourself, who do you know who is good at nurturing? Hang out with them as much as possible. First-time Mums are usually (but not always) wired to serve baby's needs first. They can be less adept at looking after themselves.

Some put pressure on themselves about media fed notions of their restored figure, baby sleeping through the night, or attending all the mother and baby groups and classes available. In many cultures, newborns and mothers do little else but spend time recovering and getting to know each other.

This post pregnancy time is called a "Confinement". Until this catches on as a cultural norm, we're often dealing with visitors from day one, some who come with suitcases showing no signs of leaving!

For this reason many new mums need help taking care of themselves where they never needed support before. It could be as simple as reassuring a mother not to feel guilty about not wanting to attend a family party and the people around her realising that she needs to simply rest.

When we give birth we can sometimes activate our own birth story too. Deep unconscious worries can bubble up to the surface quite unexpectedly so go really easy with yourself (and your birth supporter too), know that you've totally got this.

Know too that you can learn and grow through any of these deep seated worries or patterns because they are just old memories or beliefs which, when you approach it today, you have way more resources and wisdom.

Give you and your birth partner time, space and ask for what you want. Go easy on the people around you too.

When life was simpler
there was more white space in the diary

Be on guard

House moves, wedding plans, weekends away, and business trips. Being pregnant does not mean you are broken and can't do these things but REMEMBER you are also growing heart ventricles and a central nervous system and a million other things for a new human being at the same time.

It's important NOT to be constantly busy. Cortisol levels for baby get set while in the womb, they are like the revs level on a car. Your approach and the priority given to a calm environment in which baby grows has an impact on the birth and set the scene for their lifetime.

> **"Pregnancy and birth is a special time, when**
> **all reverent treatment of mother and baby will**
> **be repaid in the following chapters of life."**

Be on guard that you allow space for a new regime to get established in your life.

Examine any resistance you have about a slowing of pace, lack of attendance at certain events or declining anything that places physical demands on you and your growing family.

EXERCISE

- Is there an event you feel that you must go to?

- Are the reasons you must go, really true?

- Is there a way of getting what you want and making it less demanding of you physically, mentally or emotionally?

What is she not saying?
What's on her mind?
Find out.

Be a detective

Birth supporter! Please believe that she is strong, that she can do this. Because she really can if you support her.

Have you ever wondered what proper support looks like? Perhaps you haven't been well supported or helped much in your own life. Some upbringings can be quite harsh even if on the surface they look all rosy.

Great support for a birthing mother is crucial. It is created by giving her exactly what she needs, and by covering for the things she isn't even aware of that could make things easier for her, enhance her whole experience or her self-belief.

People with great support achieve great things.

Your support can also mean your own inner resilience (that can be restored by some rest or delegation of tasks) or a team of unconditionally supportive people who fulfil different aspects of your needs.

Also check what needs your birth supporter has as well. Who do they need to support them so you don't have to?

Are there any other needs that baby may have too?

You must seek to be compassionately decisive and extol generous leadership.

Knights (and queens) in shining armour

You are not broken faulty or difficult

Get clear about your needs and desires and share them with people closest to you. People who love and care for you will work to satisfy those needs and wants, no matter how unconventional or awkward they appear to be.

EXERCISE

How to get clear about what you need.

Imagine you have a magic wand. How would you feel if everything was perfect? What needs to happen (and what needs not to happen) if perfection and magic in this birth scenario was possible?

What don't you want (and remember your unconscious mind can't process negatives so be wary of long lists of 'don't wants'. This could be an indicator that some of your needs are not being met).

Special advice for Partners

It is likely to be necessary for you to take a stand, challenge or at least question the way things are being handled along the pregnant, birthing or parenting journey. This is your journey too and to become the sort of person your partner and children respect and admire in the long term, you will be given opportunities to demonstrate generous or compassionate leadership.

Recognise though that this might not be easy, especially when faced with a new unfamiliar situation like having a baby. It is an opportunity to create, strengthen or fortify the foundation of your relationship. Becoming reliable, trusted and elegantly protective of the birthing mother and child is key part of the long-term relationship with both mother and the child too.

You do not seek to protect the mother because she is weak, you protect her because she is important.

*"…be a sensible person,
use your voice and don't be nervous,
you can do this you've got purpose…"*

(Nahko Bear and Medicine For The People)

Be your baby's advocate

Find your voice and if you need to, stand up for the baby's experience as well as the your own.

Complaints and dissatisfaction with maternity care can arise after the event is over. Perhaps because a woman doesn't feel listened to or that she or baby hasn't been cared for in a gentle way.

Baby has just been through a scary time too, not sure about what to do, never having done this before, leaving the environment s/he's only ever known, from a warm, dark, quiet space to the (very different) outside world.

Make the experience for baby less overwhelming, keep it calm, quiet, dark and make sure s/he is kept warm and handled like a piece of precious porcelain. It may be necessary for you to find your voice to make sure that this happens.

Only the truly strong can be strong with softness and that is exactly what baby needs from everyone at their birth.

*Place one hand on your forehead and
one on the back of your head*

What to do if you start falling into fear: be double relaxed

What to do and why

The amygdala is a primitive part of the brain that is primarily concerned with survival. Some people describe it as the 'lizard brain' or the 'ape brain'. When adrenaline floods the system, the hippocampus (the day to day part of the brain) is bypassed and information about our environment is sent to the amygdala in order to determine whether to fight, flee, freeze or fawn (or something else).

If you're going into fear, I saw the following advice from Diane Speier who suggests to do the following to calm the amygdala.

EXERCISE

Place one hand over your forehead horizontally, and your other hand on the back of your head and breathe slow and steady in through your nose and out through your mouth for 3-5 minutes. This should calm things down for you. It engages neurovasculars and brings blood flow back to the frontal lobe and calms the amygdala.

Acknowledgements

There are so many people to thank for helping me get this book birthed.

A big thank you to my amazing family and all the friends whose unwavering belief in me has helped me to listen to the voice inside to keep going and ignore the naysayers to never ditch the whole idea, even against a choppy life backdrop.

The person who stands out the most is my Mum without whom my spark of self-belief in the hard won knowledge contained in this book, would have surely been snuffed out long ago.

Every day, I am grateful to my two sons who have taught and stretched me on all levels since before they were even born. Thank you for choosing me as your Mummy and for accompanying me with two very different life changing experiences of birth. You are the greatest gifts in my life and I am truly blessed to get to spend my days with both of you.

An enormous thank you also goes to the birth world; the birth keepers - the hard working, passionate midwives, ante-natal teachers, doula trainers, the charities, the independent midwives, the amazing staff and the forward thinking consultants on the maternity wards.

These people make it their life's work to improve the environments and experiences that mothers and babies have. I have learned so much from so many in the birth community and even though I'm a bit of an outsider with my business-like demeanour, they have all been really supportive of my desire to reach smart women to help them tap into, an often different set of talents as they approach motherhood. Special thanks too for the women who have videoed and shared their births so that women can see how beautiful a real birth can be.

But the biggest thanks goes to you, the reader. Thank you for choosing to read this. I know it will serve you, but if you hadn't chosen to be curious about the words written inside, then what would have been the point? Thank you and my best wishes are sent to you and all your blessed hearts during this magical time of transformation.

About the author

Marie Taylor was born in Essex in the 1970s. She grew up in the cultural soup of the stockbroker belt of the 80s. By 18 she'd broken free of Essex and was educated at Aston University's Business School in Birmingham. After graduating and holding many corporate roles a seemingly minor car accident had a profound impact. A simple but significant shunt from behind on the M1 motorway was the kick up the behind she needed to begin a domino effect of changes in her life that was the start of her exploration of the then 'new age'. Now, thirty years later these ideas are much more widely accepted and backed up with robust research.

While she forged ahead with her corporate career she was also seeking something more fulfilling that could serve the world and make a difference. She began to study communication, persuasion and influence.

This lead on to a detailed study of why people do what they do and how to help them develop beneficial behaviours and stop destructive ones that keep them from being doing or getting what they want.

Those worlds converged when she moved to Bristol, then newly qualified as a life coach, she got married and shortly after experienced a difficult transition to motherhood.

It was during this early motherhood chapter of exhaustion, isolation and recovery that the idea for Urban Earth Mother was born. The mission behind it gradually unfolded as a hub for women's wisdom that wasn't getting handed down through the generations because of the way we live in modern society. After a triumphant birth followed her first traumatic one she knew that Birth was the topic to tackle first.

Urban Earth Mother exists today to support people by connecting them to wisdom and experiences outside the mainstream.

Marie coaches and provides consulting to help women find their voice and become better leaders at home, at work and in their communities. She also supports men to be healthier, happier and have a more sustainable existence.

www.urbanearthmother.com

Reading list

Ina May's Guide to Childbirth
by Ina May Gaskin

Spiritual Midwifery
by Ina May Gaskin

Gentle Birth Method: The Month-by-Month Jeyarani Way Programme
by Dr Gowri Motha

Birth Crisis
by Sheila Kitzinger

Inducing Labour: Making Informed Decisions
by Sara Wickham

Seven Secrets of a Joyful Birth
by Dominique Sakoilsky

Getting into the Vortex
by Abraham Hicks

evidencebasedbirth.com

laleche.org.uk

postnatalangel.co.uk

doulafilm.com

doula.org.uk

aims.org.uk

sands.org.uk

Lightning Source UK Ltd.
Milton Keynes UK
UKHW020722150320
360356UK00007B/179